shoes and shopping

shoes and shopping

jo hemmings

NEW
HOLLAND

contents

introduction

Shoes and shopping. The words alone go together like a horse and carriage, Morecambe and Wise, Christmas and crap telly. A match made in retail heaven.

Shopping is the UK's most popular leisure activity and women are the leading exponents. A recent survey indicated that the contents of the average woman's wardrobe is worth around £3000, with one in six women owning more than £5000 worth of clothes and shoes. We tend to hang on to clothes even though we haven't worn them for a season. We know what goes around, comes around, and holding onto our best fashion buys will often pay huge dividends in the future, when those items come right back into fashion on the merry-go-round of taste and design.

While so many of us love to shop, some serious shopaholics actually get physical withdrawal symptoms if they are unable to shop. These symptoms include depression, heart palpitations, nausea and cold sweats. Conversely, when they are shopping, women experience sensational highs and enormous pleasure, only matched by the most exhilarating orgasm or certain illegal drugs. Scientists call this compulsive shopping behaviour 'oniomania' (from the Greek 'onios' meaning sale and 'mania' meaning, er, mania). Shopping is also a great stress buster. While some women may turn to alcohol or wild partying to relieve day-to-day stress, a significant proportion of us shop.

Thankfully most us keep our shopping habits under relative control and while we admit to frequent bouts of retail therapy and may be self-confessed shopaholics, we still manage to curb our financial urges just enough to ensure that we pay for some of the other little necessities of life like food or the mortgage.

women: born to shop

Studies have shown that women are far happier shopping than men. Especially when it comes to fashion shopping. While men will happily buy stuff online or spend hours shopping for the latest technological gadgets or computer 'add-ons', they fail miserably when it comes to fashion purchases. Firstly men express a need, rather than a want. "I need a new jumper, therefore I will go out to buy a new jumper". One or two shops later and the task is completed to their satisfaction. Women use the same expression, however this is almost always a desire, a 'want' rather than a need. "I need a new pair of shoes/pair of black trousers". No you don't. You probably have a least half a dozen, perfectly up-to-date and serviceable pairs of both. You *want* a new pair of shoes/trousers, because you

love to shop. Because it makes you feel good and has the added promise of that new pair of shoes/trousers being just a little bit more gorgeous than all the other pairs. Absolutely right – why not? We were born to shop.

Studies have shown that 72 minutes is the male boredom threshold when on a shopping expedition. The less faint-hearted woman however, can continue for another 28 minutes before she even considers calling it a day. This is in part due to our basic hunter/gatherer instincts. Traditionally men, as the hunters, go forth, find their prey and kill it. So, when they need a new black jumper, they simply go to a shop and they buy it. Hit and run stuff. Women, on the other hand, are traditionally the gatherers. They make considered choices and are happy to browse until they find what they want, often gathering other purchases along the way. This makes us less targeted and focussed in our shopping habits, than our male counterparts. However, it also makes us far better shoppers than men, taking our time to search out the bargains and find the better purchases.

In fact, women – on average – make a ten percent better cost saving than men, mainly because of our browsing instincts, rather than the mission-seeking tactics adopted by male shoppers.

bargain shopping

The word 'bargain', like the word 'sale' quickens our heart rate, makes us salivate and increases our desire to shop. We love it! But what exactly is a bargain? Let's take a dispassionate look…

• Value for money obviously. Even though studies have shown that over 40% of 'bargains' are actually items sold at a shop's standard retail price!

• The best bargains are a balance between the perceived cost saving and the level of desire for an item.

• This desire is driven by a combination of an item's perceived value or use, the length of time we have wanted this item and its perceived rarity or availability.

These factors drive us towards getting value for money and increase our spending power. Basically you get more for your money! This is one of the reasons why outlet shopping, warehouse sales and shopping chains such as TK Maxx have taken Britain by storm in the last decade or so.

consuming passion

What exactly is it that makes us love shopping so much? And why, as this book shows, do so many of us target shoes and other accessories as our favoured objects of desire? Shopping for ourselves – which means fashion shopping rather than shopping for items for our home or present buying – is a huge mood lifter. If we feel down about life, then a little retail therapy can have a miraculous and almost immediate effect on our attitude to life.

Alternatively, if we are feeling good about life, then a serious shopping bout is an affirmation and a celebration of that mood. In business-speak this is a 'Win/Win' situation!

Almost every occasion demands a shopping trip. A special night out? A new dress/pair of shoes/handbag/jewellery. An interview? New suit. Just joined the gym? New workout gear/trainers. First date? New outfit/makeup. Going on holiday? New swimwear. New season? More clothes… Just how good does life get?

Women are clever about shopping too. While in our teens we may have gone for high fashion – of the here today, gone tomorrow sort – and shopped at Top Shop, River Island or New Look, as we approach our twenties and thirties and beyond, we move on. We get a taste for designer goods, we get to know the lay-out of our local department store like the back of our hand and we get to know just what suits us and accentuates our good features, while disguising the bad.

Fashion is a wonderful thing. We learn that rather than striving to keep up with all the latest trends, we can adapt our existing wardrobe with the handbag of the moment or just an accent touch of the latest colour. While black will always be the new black, slimming and flattering as it is to almost all of us, we learn to add touches of colour or a brilliant piece of jewellery and learn that spending a fortune on a seriously expensive winter coat is the best investment that there is.

We love shoes, jewellery, handbags and cosmetics. Like hats, scarves and gloves, accessories are the most forgiving of items. No struggling with zips, VPL or unsightly bulges. Bliss…

sex and shopping

Sex and shopping have long been recognized as the perfect match. Both, when good, are immensely pleasurable, calorie free and deeply satisfying. But they are even more closely matched than this. Scientists claim that the scent of a sexy man can trigger a shopping spree. Male pheromones – those scents that our conscious mind is unaware of, but can drive us crazy with sexual desire – apparently send subliminal messages to our unconscious mind and drive us to shop. It has even been suggested that these pheromones could be pumped through a shop's air conditioning systems in order to drive us into a shopping frenzy!

Other surveys have shown that women actually prefer shopping to sex. A recent poll of 1000 people showed that 52% of women would rather go shopping than make love. On the other hand – and not surprisingly – 93% of men were shown to prefer sex to shopping!

shoes and shopping

This book is all about you. Looking at the shopping obsessions of a variety of women, throughout Great Britain, all shopping life is revealed within these

pages. Collections don't just include shoes –
but also boots, handbags and belts; perfume,
nail varnish, jewellery and leather. There are
market shoppers, vintage shoppers, online
shoppers and charity shop shoppers. And
much more. It is about women who have
found their fashion nirvana, know what looks
good on them and will go to any lengths to
add another item to their collection. These
brave women have opened up their hearts and
their collections for you to take a peek inside.
Every one of you will have a similar collection
of your own. It may be earrings or necklaces,
suede trousers or satin skirts, killer heels or
designer trainers; eye shadows, lipsticks or
moisturisers. It's there somewhere, lurking
in the recesses of your wardrobe or your
make-up bag and each and every collection
is a celebration of the diversity of style unique
to women and our unashamed love of
retail therapy.

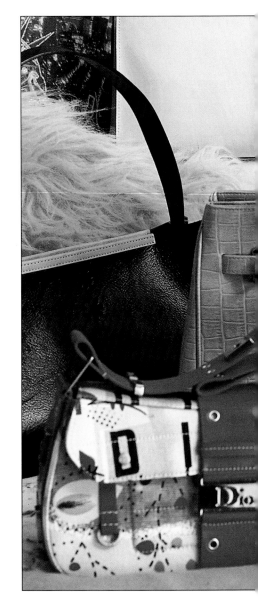

dressed to the nineties

Linzi's passion is for vintage clothes. Not just any clothes but beautiful, glamorous, sexy and feminine suits and dresses. "My special favourites are vintage dresses from the '50s and '60s and many of my best finds have come straight out of my mother's wardrobe!"

As someone who has worked in the fashion industry since she was 14, owning her own clothes store at 18 and footwear company at 22, Linzi has the privilege of previewing fashion collections six months before they hit the shops and can plan her wardrobe of summer dresses in the gloom of mid-winter.

Her spending patterns can vary from next-to-nothing in one month to £2000 in a single day! Working in the heart of London's West End can prove to be an expensive temptation. "But I buy very carefully and avoid the here today, gone tomorrow, cutting edge fashion."

"I may be extravagant but these vintage clothes have already passed the test of time."

get ahead – get a hat

Fiona has loved hats for as long as she can remember. She's lucky enough to have the kind of face that suits most styles of hat and is forever buying them – mainly in charity shops and department store sales.

Practical as well as gorgeous – we lose up to 90% of our body heat through our heads – she also believes that they finish off an outfit in a way that no other accessory can. They are also great fun and often a talking point.

"My favourite shop is Accessorize, but I do while away many a lunch hour trying on the oh-so gorgeous but oh-so expensive hats in the department stores in Oxford Street." While she can't afford most of them, they do provide inspiration for her bargain buys.

Fiona has collected hats from as far afield as Latvia, Australia and Vietnam and is always happy to receive them as presents, however eclectic the colour or style.

"There's something about a woman in a hat that makes her that little bit different. I'd describe it as a warm-headed expression!"

bargain hunting double act

Rosina and Ruth make a formidable, bargain hunting, mother and daughter double act. Both adore the buzz of market shopping – as much for the bargains to be found there as for the sheer camaraderie between the stallholders and the shoppers.

Their shared enthusiasm has clearly been passed down the generations, with Rosina's own mother being a keen market shopper. Ruth admits she shops as often as she can "spending wildly fluctuating amounts" depending on how much money she has. They both believe that shopping lifts their mood, "it's as if endorphins are released in your body".

Ruth loves Portobello Market – especially for vintage clothes – designer sample sales, charity shops and TK Maxx. "In Portobello Market you can buy clothes from designers who are just starting out. In a couple of years they might just be the darlings of London Fashion Week."

While Rosina used to spend "ridiculous amounts of money" on dresses from seminal designers of the '60s and '70s, like Ossie Clarke and Mary Quant, these days she spends most of her money at Leeds market – mainly on bags, jewellery and boots.

Rosina " There's no skill in wandering down Bond Street, with a limitless credit card – any fool can do that".

a shine for shoes

Janie's passion for shoes isn't just restricted to her own vast collection of over 100 pairs. As a young child she recalls being enthralled by other people's shoes too. She was fascinated by her babysitter's white wedges decorated with "beautiful clouds along the sides" as well as Uncle Michael's stylish cream brogues. Even her Wellington boots were customized with transfers and ribbons. "I even had a special name for them – 'Ebbies'."

Shopping mostly for kitten heels and vintage-style winkle-pickers, rather than sandals, "I'm not keen on feet", Janie's funkiest shoes include green hand-beaded slippers with turned up toes and cream leather cowboy style boots – "the leg of the boot is cut out to resemble lace". Best bargains include "disco diva silver party shoes embellished with pink and green stripes" bought for a less than diva-ish £10 and a pair of red crochet high heels, bought for a similar sum.

Janie gets inspiration for her collection from the big designer names: Prada, Jimmy Choo, Gina, Christian Laboutin and Chanel are amongst her favourites. She then heads for the sales or the high street outlets for more affordable versions.

"My dream – which will become a reality – is to own a shoe shop called 'Foxy Feet'. But, I do see the dangers in that…"

help! i'm a label victim

Laura is the ultimate shopahaolic. Not content with high street brands and chain store copies, Laura has to have the real thing, spending at least £200 a month on her heart's desires.

"After I spent to the limit a couple of years ago, I was forced to cut up my credit card to prevent any further abuse." Although she's a little more careful now, she still shops during most lunchtimes saving herself for a 'big shop' at the weekend. She's immensely proud of her collection of designer labels, and loves the special feeling of both buying and wearing them. So precious are her clothes and accessories that she has even insured them for £7000!

She adores her Chanel sunglasses, earrings and bracelet as well as her collection of Tiffany jewellery and is anticipating the imminent purchase of a special edition Louis Vuitton handbag. More than anything though, she covets a pair of gorgeous Jimmy Choo shoes, costing an eye-watering £700.

"When I start shopping, I just can't stop. It's almost as though someone else takes over my body!"

brief encounter

Like so many of us, Louise believes that wearing gorgeous underwear makes us feel good, even if it is only our outer layer that is on show. While a great pair of pants can hold us in, out or up wherever we choose and the right bra can add inches and shape to our natural assets, knowing that we are wearing sexy underwear is a good feeling in itself.

"I would never leave home without matching underwear," says Louise, who often buys underwear when she's feeling low, has somewhere special to go – or just because.

A keen bargain hunter, she favours Selfridges lingerie department or holiday purchases, where she can buy something special and unique. It's not just about lacy bra and pants sets either – Louise's collection includes some "hugely extravagant and exclusive" fishnet stockings bought in Milan as well as a black PVC set courtesy of Ann Summers.

"It's a matter of personal pride to wear matching underwear. It's also that 'just might get run over by a bus' scenario that we all worry about."

kiss and make up

Phoebe has a serious addiction to buying cosmetics. And not just your run-of-the-mill variety either. She adores creating her image with wild colours and textures, although does confess to possessing literally hundreds of designer products from the likes of Chanel and Nars, costing a fortune, but never used. Perhaps understandably then, Phoebe is reluctant to reveal just how much she spends each month on her obsession, but admits to never being in credit.

"My fascination with beauty products started as a young child. I managed to persuade my father to spend a small fortune on Clarins products for my mother, knowing full well that she didn't use the range and that it would all be passed on to me!"

Phoebe shops every single day and in fact once had counselling for her shopping addiction. While she couldn't bring herself to actually stop shopping, she now indulges her urges by buying vast quantities of nail varnishes and lipsticks – again, most never worn.

"I love to shop online and Direct Cosmetics, www.directcosmetics.com, is my favourite site." Here she can buy all of her favourite goodies for a fraction of the recommended retail price.

"My obsession started when I was five. I mixed my mother's Chanel No. 5 with crushed rose petals from the garden. I got a good smack."

we loved shopping so much, we bought the shop…

Tamara and Emma share both a background in the fashion industry as well as a love of shopping. Now they run Mee (which means 'beautiful' in Chinese) a unique one-stop fashion, beauty, accessories and lifestyle boutique based in Bath.

"Our fashion addiction started when we were nine and coveted Olivia Newton-John's skin-tight, shiny black trousers as worn by her character, Sandy, in Grease." While Tamara's trouser envy was rewarded with a pair of yellow footless tights, poor Emma received nothing.

They are both crazy about shoes – especially Jimmy Choos, Prada and Terry de Havilland – as well as luxurious and self-indulgent fabrics like chiffon and lace.

Having a personal shopping expenditure of around £150 a month each, they both confess to being constantly tempted by everything in their shop as each item sold in Mee is personally chosen by the two of them.

"There's something about new clothes that makes you think that they will change your life. But it only lasts for a couple of weeks and then you're onto the next thing."

top totty

"I have over 100 tops and T-shirts in my collection." Hannah believes that they are the most versatile type of clothing – as well as being relatively cheap and immediately noticeable. Customizing tops is fun too – Hannah has been known to write on them, cut them up and add her own personal touches such as buckles on the shoulder, sequins and mismatching buttons.

"As a child, my mother owned a long, fitted waistcoat that I loved. That's what started my obsession…" Now she shops five times a week, plus a few more times via the internet, and most of her monthly budget of £200 is spent on tops and T-shirts. "My favourite shops include Top Shop, FCUK and Affleck's Palace in Manchester." Top websites – especially for the more eclectic style Hannah favours – include www.djtees.com and www.davidandgoliath.com.

While she loves to find a bargain in the sales – who doesn't? – her favourite tops are those that attract the most compliments. She also goes for funky colours to ring the changes and a favourite is a bubblegum pink and maroon jumper from Soochi. Other more eccentric items include a red and black striped vest top, with skull and crossbones – again picked out in those ubiquitous sequins!

"Tops can speak to you somehow, they express a part of who I am."

charity begins near home

Wendy chanced upon the joys of charity shopping, when some years ago she dropped off some of her own clothes at a local charity shop, instead of taking them to the local refuse tip. She was amazed to find good quality clothes with well-known labels from high street names at knockdown prices.

Spending as little as £5 a month, her big bargain was a Musto showerproof jacket, normally retailing for £99, selling for £7.50. Another major purchase was a still labelled and unworn Country Casuals jacket for £3. "My most extravagant item was a sheepskin coat, bought in Frinton-on-Sea for the less-than-princely sum of £12."

At these prices Wendy can afford to indulge her more eccentric shopping fantasises, including zebra print leggings and a pair of pink leather Dr Marten boots.

Never one to let an opportunity or a bargain pass her by, Wendy can usually be found in her local charity shop on a Saturday morning, while taking a quick break from looking after her horse, stabled close by.

"My husband thinks that I'm absolutely disgusting for buying 'someone else's clothes' and won't let me go near a charity shop when we're out together."

these boots were made for walking

Maria admits to having an almost physical addiction to boots. The 'must-have' butterflies-in-the-pit-of-her-stomach factor simply takes over, irrespective of price, and like so many shopaholics, she gets a real high as she leaves a shop with yet another pair of boots. "I even get withdrawal symptoms if I'm away from my beloved Selfridges shoe department for too long!"

Maria's first pair of boots were of the suede pixie variety, bought for her twelfth birthday. She wore them with pride and so her love affair began. "While I recently donated 10 pairs of platform-soled, block-heeled and round-toed boots to my local charity shop, I do normally find it heartbreaking to part with any of my collection!"

Spending around £200 a month on boots – with a shopping expedition most weekends – she now favours pointy toes and stiletto heels on her boot buying forays. Her most extravagant buy was a pair of frighteningly expensive bright pink patent leather three-quarter length boots with seriously pointed toes. The pink theme continues with her best bargain to date – a dusky pink suede pair, embellished with daisies: a much-more-expensive looking pair which cost Maria only £20.

"My boots make me so happy. I sometimes just spend five minutes gazing at them to cheer me up after a bad day at work."

jean genie

Joanna's passion is for all things denim. As a recent Miss Leeds, she confesses to being something of a tomboy when younger and her love affair with denim started when she was just 11. When boot cut jeans came into vogue, the love affair became a permanent one.

Whole Saturdays are spent in Leeds pursuing her passion with favourite shops being Republic, Top Shop and the Corn Exchange. Favourite jeans include huge flares and embroidered jeans, but denim bags feature large in her collection too.

"Top Shop jeans are cute and funky and they cater for slim people with long legs – gotta love 'em!"

"Denim can be dressed up or down, goes with everything and never goes out of fashion"

from lulu to louis

Even though Laura is still studying, she has a passion for designer handbags. By shopping in the sales, designer outlets, charity shops and on internet auctions, she manages to find plenty of bargains.

"I started collecting designer handbags when I bought a gorgeous Lulu Guinness handbag in New York and her shop in Belgravia is a special place for me." Although she did manage to buy a Lulu Guinness embroidered purse in a charity shop in London for a fraction of its original price. Her favourite bag is made by Christian Dior – a pink, blue and white confection, bought as a gift for her 18th birthday.

She loves to shop in Covent Garden, Camden Market and regularly walks the length of Oxford Street in search of her beloved designer handbags. Not all of her handbags have top designer names though – she's happy to buy something she really loves by lesser-known names too.

"I love the way designer bags have their own special dust covers to keep them protected, each with their own designer logo."

going, going, gone…

Lucy loves the anticipation of buying clothes on eBay. She says that "it combines the thrill of an auction with the excitement of discovering something unique". The real buzz comes when auctions are coming to an end and there's a bidding frenzy in the last few moments before the sale closes.

Lucy is a huge fan of vintage clothing from the '40s and '50s – suiting her enviable hourglass figure – and she fell upon eBay's huge collection of vintage clothing while looking for Marc Jacobs's designer items. eBay's virtual treasure trove offers everything from dresses, coats and blouses to jewellery, shoes, handbags and scarves to complete the authentic look.

Spending up to £200 per month, Lucy finds it easy to justify her expenditure, as anything that she tires of, simply gets recycled and sold onto another keen collector, via eBay of course.

Vintage bargains include "an extravagantly beaded cardigan, from the '50s, which came all the way from Utah in the USA" as well as a pair of long beaded gloves – also from the '50s – and a fully reversible oriental jacket. All this for a mere £35.

"eBay is deliciously virtual and completely addictive."

suits you, madam

Helen is both a personal shopper (www.yessyess.com) and a model for a local department store in Glasgow, so is never short of opportunities to indulge her passion for buying jackets and suits.

She's happy to pay £300 for a great suit and match it up with a top for a fiver, believing that the look is then both classy and effective. "If there's a bargain to be found in my local department store, I'll find it or the staff will advise me. Isn't life great!"

"I prefer classic clothes to the latest fads, although I once bought a beautiful blue fox fur jacket while living in Canada, only to promptly sell it on my return to Scotland, because I was somewhat concerned about the reactions of animal activists."

Lucky Helen has a supportive husband who often encourages her to go out and buy herself a new jacket or suit, so combined with her job it's no surprise that she has such a huge number of jackets in her wardrobe.

"Like all shopaholics I just have to buy a jacket or suit that I fancy, whenever and wherever I happen to be."

glove actually

Gloves epitomize ultimate elegance to Charlotte. "Just like Jackie O, I think that they 'finish off' an outfit and add a special sophistication and style."

However, Charlotte's glove affair started way back, with a rather less elegant image – woolly mittens knitted by her grandmother! Graduating through the '80s fad for fingerless gloves, she has progressed through long satin gloves, vintage '50s gloves and is now into beautiful soft leather gloves in a wide range of colours, including shocking pink which co-ordinates perfectly with her matching clothes collection.

Spending up to £50 a month, rarely a week goes by without another pair of gloves being added to her collection. Her best buy so far must be a pair of eccentric black leather gloves with a red rabbit-fur cuff, reduced from £75 to £18 in last winter's Fortnum and Mason sale.

Life is not all luxury, however, as Charlotte loves to buy gloves in second-hand shops too and the Salvation Army has been a happy hunting ground!

"I really got into gloves for practical reasons – my hands are always freezing!"

heaven scent

Lesley is an avid collector of perfume. Her obsession lies in emotional reminiscences – "just putting on a particular fragrance takes me back to a particular moment in time – what I was doing, wearing, who I was with and what record was playing".

She loved the scents that the older girls wore at school – it made them seem so "grown up" while Lesley wore cheaper, less sophisticated fragrances like Cachet, Geminesse or Smitty. She recalls that her first 'grown-up' scent was Paris by Yves St Laurent, so powerful that she was banned from wearing it indoors, "you could practically taste it!"

Lesley shops weekly to add to her collection and currently has 36 different bottles of scent. She loves buying perfume in the grand fragrance halls of Harvey Nichols and Harrods and also has many unusual perfumes which she has brought back from overseas trips – Jean Louis Scherrer, Marroussia and Castelbajac are just some of the fragrances that most of us won't have heard of.

She adores new fragrances and reckons that she has "a nose for smells". In fact Lesley is known for her innate ability to recognize a scent "at fifty paces".

"Thierry Mugler's 'Angel' is my signature scent. I bought it back from Dallas in 1993, when it wasn't available in Britain. I'm gutted now that you can get it in Superdrug."

professional bargain hunter

Noelle began her bargain hunting 'career' around 25 years ago, while working at Cosmopolitan magazine. "I fell upon my first designer sample sale, at Paul Costelloe in the heart of the rag trade in London, at about the same time as my Editor politely suggested that it was time I moved on from Miss Selfridge to something a little classier, fashion-wise." Having triumphed through the crowds to buy three designer outfits at her first sale, she soon became addicted, relying on the shopping grapevine to discover yet more of these, rarely advertised, designer sales.

Now running her own factory shopping website, www.gooddealdirectory.co.uk, as well organising eight consumer shows a year, she rarely visits the high street and never pays full price for anything in her wardrobe. Her greatest bargain was a sheepskin coat, reduced in a fashion sale from £1200 to £550. And as if that wasn't enough, she later saw it in Harrods for nearly £3000!

"Born to shop, forced to work. That's me."

top of the shops

Kelly-Jae is addicted to Top Shop's flagship store at Oxford Circus. As one of the earliest stores to copy catwalk designs, Kelly-Jae can be found checking out the new stock every Thursday night and Saturday morning. And between times she's also seeking out those new arrivals at her local branch.

"I'm especially fond of the limited edition and vintage sections and I own the basic Top Shop vest in every available colour and style." And in case you think Top Shop's the cheaper end of the market, Kelly-Jae has managed to spend £300 in one hit on a vintage suede jacket.

Spending between £500 and £800 every month at Top Shop, Kelly-Jae's shopping philosophy is follow your instincts fashion-wise, don't be dictated to by others. "I have learned to accept my addiction, rather than try to fight it. As long as I get my fix I am happy, try to keep me away and I get cold turkey!"

"Wear whatever makes you feel good and never ask for a second opinion!"

a major blonde moment

Charlotte is a dedicated follower of fashion – in a Barbie meets Britney way. It began with buying a Britney Spears type hat, then a Britney coat and suddenly Charlotte was having a major blonde moment. She even buys Barry M cosmetics and wears Britney's favourite perfume to complete the look.

Working in shopping paradise – London's Oxford Street – she confesses to going shopping every single day spending almost all of her money on clothes and accessories. Bargains include a pair of Barbie style cowboy boots, reduced from £110 to £40.

Like her style icon Britney, Charlotte is highly individual in her taste and how she wears her clothes. She once shocked fellow prom goers by wearing a thrown-together, cut-up silk dress rather than the more traditional ball gown. Never one to care about other people's attitudes, Charlotte says she "once cut up a man's shirt and made it into a boob tube. The sleeves were leg warmers and the collar was a necklace!"

"My motto is to follow your heart and wear whatever makes you happy."

an especially fine vintage

Laura has had a passion for antique fairs and markets from a tender age and it seemed inevitable that her taste and enthusiasm should progress to a love of vintage clothes. While fashions come and go and come again and high street chains strain to keep up with the trends, Laura simply visits vintage clothing shops and fairs and buys the originals.

It's not an expensive option and Laura manages to spend less than £30 a month on her obsession. By shopping every Saturday, she's often first in line for the best bargains. "The Battersea Vintage Fashion Fair and local charity shops are particular favourites, but I've recently discovered the pleasures of buying online and have just bagged myself a vintage coat from Chloe on eBay."

Other special items include an eccentric faux fur coat and a Gucci handbag bought for a bargain $10 in a New York thrift store.

"You have to be quick. If you spot a special item, you have to get it there and then or you miss it."

retail therapy is just a mouse click away

Danielle's online shopping addiction really kicked in when high-speed broadband made the pleasure even faster. As someone who's always short of time, surfing the net provides the ultimate shopping nirvana. She shops for almost all her clothes online, although draws the line at buying shoes over the net.

Spending around £1000 a month – and sometimes twice that amount – Danielle devotes at least half of that to buying her designer fashion online. She even loves sending clothes back if not suitable and seeing the credit go back onto her card!

While some of the best sites are American, the hassle of shipping the goods across the Atlantic and the variation in American sizing policy makes her favour UK sites. Her favourites include www.bravissimo.com for lingerie, especially as everything arrives beautifully packed in tissue and bows and www.netaporter.com for its great choice of designer collections. As a curvy 32DD, she hates trying on underwear in shops, so she also loves www.agentprovocateur.com and www.victoriassecret.com. "I await the arrival of Madame V lingerie online in the UK with baited breath."

"As well as the delicious pleasure of being able to shop in the middle of the night, I absolutely adore receiving the beautiful packages."

the painted lady

"Buying a new nail varnish is one of the cheapest ways to make yourself feel good and give yourself a treat at the same time", says Rebecca from personal experience. She started collecting nail varnish in her first job, when she was paid little more than a pittance. While watching her friends treat themselves to clothes galore, she simply went out and added another bottle to her collection. She reckons she now has well over 100 bottles to choose from.

Spending around £20 a month on nail varnish, she pops out once or twice a week to add to her collection. Ranging from a humble Rimmel pot at less than a quid, she also loves Chanel's Rouge Noir – made famous by Uma Thurman in the film *Pulp Fiction* – which costs more than ten times that much! Her favourite make is Boots No 7 – a huge range and virtually chip free.

With all of those bottles to choose from it's not surprising that Rebecca likes two-colour designs. Her current favourite is a 'reverse' French manicure with a red base and blue-black tips.

"It's important that my toe nails are always immaculate too – I wouldn't want to have nasty yellow hooves!"

high on style, low on cash

Katie loves outlet shopping and prides herself on never paying the full recommended retail price for any of her clothes collection. By mixing designer styles, one-offs and catwalk samples with high-street fashion, she has created a unique and funky look.

"As a teenager I became adept at stretching pocket money, wherever possible, to indulge my passion for clothes and the habit has stayed with me." Currently spending around £350 a month her favourite bargain hunting grounds are quarterly designer warehouse sales in London and TK Maxx. However, in the cloak and dagger and highly competitive world of the stylish bargain hunter, Katie refuses to reveal her top source of designer samples!

Even though her best bargain has only managed to have one outing so far, she's especially proud of her navy, full-length Ralph Lauren ball gown bought at TK Maxx in New York for $120 (about £75). Another unusual item is a long purple Sue Rowe coat, bought in the early '90s.

"My favourite place is The Designer Worx Sale in a photographic studio in Kings Cross (but don't tell anyone!)."

bargain basement babe

There's a bargain hunter in all of us, but Lucy has made it her specialist shopping subject. Her philosophy is to take every possible opportunity to shop – however brief and however unlikely the location or timing may seem. "Shopping is like a recreational drug!"

While charity shops offer the most extreme bargains – a vintage Lanvin couture silk suit for £45 and an Aquascutum coat for £12 – she also managed to find a Marni evening dress in Fenwicks reduced from an unreachable £450 to a somewhat more attainable £65.

Prime bargain hunting territories include high fashion chains such as H & M, Zara, Mango, MK One and Primark where the markdowns can be huge. At the other end of the scale, shopping overseas can prove fruitful too, a hand-tailored silk dress from Singapore was a relatively affordable £150, though something of an extravagance on Lucy's budget.

"But bargain hunting is mentally stimulating as well as financially draining. Looking at what's in store is like going to a design gallery – colour, shape, function, era, context and subtext – it's all there."

"Each new bargain just leads me to keep on shopping…"

best foot forward

Ghislaine – like so many of us – has an obsession with footwear. She believes that there is nothing sexier or more empowering than a great pair of shoes and believes that a passion for shoes and boots "is part of a woman's genetic makeup".

Ghislaine's mother had an amazing collection of seriously high-heeled shoes, which were coveted by her as a child. While her sister's feet grew too large for them, Ghislaine's petite feet were perfectly formed to take over the shoes when her mother tired of them.

Spending around £300 a month, Ghislaine spurns the high street chains, preferring to buy her shoes in Harrods and Harvey Nichols or as far afield as the USA and Canada. She favours Prada for most of her shoes and boots, "loving the ways that designers play with historical or exotic forms" to create their footwear. However her best bargain – reduced by a massive 80% – is a pair of Christian Dior knee-high black stiletto-heeled boots, which lace up both at the front and at the back. Another favourite – and eccentric – style is a pair of pink lizard-skin stiletto boots with brown-tooled leather toes – "a witty and expensive take on a cowboy boot".

"I so love Prada. How could anyone resist a pair of green leather boots covered all over in appliquéd leaves and beetles?"

more than skin deep

As the author of this book and a self-confessed shopaholic, I have a rather worryingly large number of collections, including enough pairs of black leather boots to fill a branch of Russell and Bromley as well as belts, coats, handbags. The list goes on…

I love leather. Not in the dominatrix sense, but as a buttermilk-soft, eminently versatile and practical fabric. Leaving aside the leather boots, handbags, belts, sofas, cushions and even my gorgeous leather bed, my wardrobe contains eight leather coats and jackets and a couple of pairs of leather and suede trousers. However, my greatest love is my collection of leather and suede skirts.

At the time of writing, I have a terrifying 18 leather and suede skirts, from soft and comfortable black leather skirts of varying lengths to absurdly impractical cream leather and purple suede numbers.

A number of my skirts are from Turkey, where specialist shops will make you a customized leather skirt for a tiny price. TK Maxx is another wonderful source of suede and leather with the added thrill of buying a designer version at a bargain basement price.

"My real passion is for leather. Bitter chocolate brown or black for winter and burnt orange, ivory and caramel for when the weather is warmer."

bagging a bargain

Louise's passion for shopping for handbags started at just seventeen. "For the first time, I could wear my own clothes and accessories to sixth-form college and I realised that handbags were the perfect way to make an outfit more individual." Her collection of handbags also suits all her changing moods from small and delicate when in a ladylike mood, to huge and oversized when chilling out in the comfort zone.

Shopping at least twice a week – not counting a daily online browse – Louise spends around £60 a month on bags and purses. An added bonus is that there's never any need to cram into sweaty changing rooms to try them on. While her most extravagant item is a Louis Vuitton bag for £300, bought when feeling low, her best bargain was a Billy Bag, reduced to a third of its original £149 price ticket.

Favourite hunting grounds include Hennes, Topshop and Warehouse, but for real individuality Louise buys most of her bags overseas, keeping a keen eye open for new lines and seasonal trends.

"A bag will never let you down, even on your 'fat' days."

shoes in the city

Carla is another one of those obsessive shoppers, who became so enthusiastic about her passion, that she opened her own shoe emporium, Shoes in the City, in the heart of Glasgow.

Carla's shoe fixation began as a young child when she insisted on wearing black patent, heeled court shoes with a gold bow – "her special Sunday shoes" – to school. She even remembers, with some embarrassment, stealing a pair of way-too-small pink shoes from her cousin's house, just because she loved them.

As well as changing her shoes up to four times a day, until she opened her own shop, she would buy shoes before work and then go back in her lunch time to buy another pair. A self-confessed "shoe junkie" she spent over £300 a month at the height of her obsession. "When I was unemployed, it meant no more shoes for a while. One day I cracked and spent my car insurance money on five pairs in one day."

She especially loves those sexy, high-heeled shoes, so beloved by Carrie and her friends in Sex in the City. Now that she owns her own shop the hardest part is having to part with anything to sell to her customers, but that just means more money for shoes of her own.

"My favourite is anything seriously glamorous, deeply impractical, that shows off a little toe cleavage."

all that glitters…

Anne loves all jewellery whether it's a humble pair of junk shop earrings or the finest white gold necklace – "you can spend £1 or £1m and still have something beautiful and unique". Spending around £70 a month on her extensive collection, she recalls that her love of all things glittery began with a gift from her parents of a gold ring, once owned by her grandmother, that was made from an old hatpin now fashioned into the letter 'A'.

She shops weekly to feed her ever-growing collection – "I love to pick up trinkets to match my latest outfit or complement my nail design" – but favours buying special items from countries as far afield as Thailand and Brazil.

Bargains include a pair of silver earrings bought for 50p while on holiday in Koh Samui. Meant to last the duration of her holiday, they are still going strong 18 months later!

Really special items include her white gold engagement ring, which fits together with a matching yellow gold wedding ring. "This is my second set of wedding/engagement rings, however I'm delighted to say that I'm still on husband number one!"

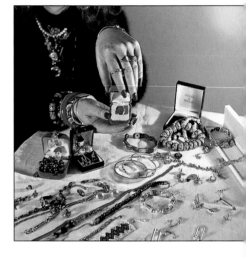

"I love jewellery, it's just like giving a Christmas tree its sparkle when the decorations are up and the lights switched on."

tighten your belt

Belts are Jo's passion. She reckons that a distinctive belt is one of the easiest and cheapest ways to maximize the impact of an outfit as well as alter the style. "While a belt slung low on the hips emphasizes and elongates the lower body making your waist look smaller, a waist clinching belt shows off the curves from shoulder to hip."

"As a teenager, I loved the 'Sam Brown' belt – a complicated confection of double leather straps", one of which apparently circled the waist, while the other crossed the torso and over the shoulder. In the '80s she collected wide, patent belts, which countered the Dynasty-style shoulder pads of the period.

These days Jo goes for a classier look, favouring good quality leather belts and Italian fabric belts. Spending around £50 a month on her collection, she is especially partial to Otto Glanz belts, but her budget usually dictates more modest designer copies from New Look and Dorothy Perkins.

Favourite belts include one bought a decade ago. Made up of rows of soft leather strands held together with a gold clasp, it features unusual hanging charms including the comedy and tragedy theatre masks.

"Precocious enough to read Vogue at 16, I realised that although the outfits and jewellery featured were too expensive, the belts were just about affordable."

mirror, mirror, on the wall…

As a student of fashion journalism, Gemma's friends are often surprised by the fact that she gets as much fun out of buying cosmetics as she does clothes. She thinks nothing of having twelve different green eyeshadows or a bathroom full of different soaps.

"I'm a keen bargain hunter, so I blag samples off the haughty cosmetics queens at make-up counters whenever possible." Her monthly spend always includes the basics like shampoo, conditioner and soap plus the extravagances of yet more perfume, scented bath oil and her particular weakness – gold lip gloss.

"My favourite product is Elizabeth Arden 8 Hour Cream, which works miracles on skin and lips." Lush shops are another fragrant hunting ground for Gemma and she's working her way through their entire product range.

Gemma readily admits to being obsessed with beauty products, and while she may have moved on from her crazy purchases that included buttercup yellow nail varnish, black lipstick and silver glitter mascara, rarely a week goes past without further indulgence.

"I was about seven years old when I got hold of the pink eyeshadow from my mum's Mary Quant make-up palette. It all went downhill from there."

the mistress of mix 'n' match

Pat absolutely adores the thrill of mixing seriously expensive designer labels with the cheap 'n' cheerful. "While some of my designer clothes and accessories are good copies, other carefully selected items are the genuine article." By wearing a faux Cartier watch, with a genuine Louis bag, a top from Primark and trousers from Zara, for instance, she can look a million dollars for a fraction of the price.

As a fitness trainer, Pat reckons that shopping is the best stress buster there is. "I spend around £250 a month and I shop pretty much every other day. My designer collection even includes an Armani coat reduced from £600 to £150." Such is her addiction that, like so many of us, she owns items that she adores but just hasn't got around to actually wearing. These include a silver sequin dress from Asda and a pair of Donna Karan shoes.

From the sublime to the ridiculous Pat's favourite shops include Gucci and Armani, as well as Zara, Primark, Peacocks and Asda!

"When I get the mix just right, the feeling is so good, it's almost physical."

beads, baubles and bangles

Steph loves all sorts of accessories. Handbags, shoes, belts, scarves, jewellery, cosmetics, even relaxation masks – she's an avid collector of just about everything and anything. "It's a girlie thing, accessories are the best possible way of standing out from the crowd."

"I made my first bead necklace at four years old, but after ending up in the local casualty department with a bead lodged up my nose, I decided it was easier to purchase my collection ready-made!"

Steph says that "life is just one big dressing up box" but she won't say how much she spends on her fabulous collection. She shops just about as often as she can, frequently taking extra suitcases on holiday, so she bring them back chock full of any accessories she can find. Her mother shares her passion, and Steph was brought up to believe that it's a no pain, no gain world if you want to be one of the beautiful people. That will account for the 'must-have' Gucci boots that Steph loves so much – gorgeous, but at least a size too small!

"I think being female is just the best stroke of luck. Thank you God for making me a girl!"

the refund queen

The temptations of shopping are huge for all of us and especially so for Aoine, working in the heart of Covent Garden. While some of us may spend too much and regret it later, particularly when the credit card bill hits the door mat, Aoine has found a way to fuel her shopping addiction and yet remain relatively solvent.

She shops almost every day, and while keeping a number of items, she returns the rest for a refund. She actually enjoys the refund experience, perhaps not a bad thing as her favourite shopping indulgence is pink shoes!

She's happy to shop anywhere and everywhere, but is especially fond of John Smedley sales and Burberry's. She receives a lot of clothes as gifts too, apparently being very easy to buy for, though presumably, only if the items come with their original receipt...

"I simply buy clothes and accessories, satisfying my craving, only to return to the shop within 28 days for a full refund."

they call her second hand rose…

Pat is the ultimate bargain hunter, scouring Glasgow's flea markets for the second-hand, previously owned and vintage bargains, especially accessories. "Other favourite haunts of mine are Brixton and Brick Lane Markets in London, as well as the flea markets of New York and Paris." See www.glasgowwestend.co.uk for her guide to shopping in Glasgow.

Just like any collector, much of her pleasure lies in the thrill of the chase, the unexpected find and the sheer joy of coming across the 'very thing' at just the right price.

As a student and a single mother, she had to eke out a minimal income in her twenties and her addiction began with that perennial favourite of the bargain hunter – jumble sales. She then went on to run stalls, selling retro jewellery and accessories at Glasgow's two famous flea markets: the Brigate (Paddy's Market) and the Barras.

Spending as little as £5 and as much as £50, she still visits the Brigate at least once a month. "Shawls, wraps and scarves are my particular trademark and I am especially fond of an exquisite lace and diamonte scarf bought for only £2."

"I have a penchant for baby shawls, which make fabulous wraps and scarves."

pink is the colour of passion

Kellie is totally obsessed with the colour pink. Girlie and feminine, she admits to wearing at least one pink item virtually every time she goes out. "I can't imagine a shopping expedition without coming home with something – anything – pink."

Her obsession covers the whole pink spectrum from baby pastel pink through to shocking pink and cerise, although Kellie favours the more muted pinks as the basis for her wardrobe.

From handbags to trousers, boots to underwear, Kellie's wardrobe is literally a riot of pink. While managing to survive on a student income of around £30 a week, she still manages to spend around £80 to £100 per month on her pink passion. Bargains include a pair of cerise leather stilettos and pink jeans from River Island, embellished with pink jewels down the side of the legs.

Nothing escapes Kellie's pink world and she even managed to find a pair of practical Timberland boots – in pink suede of course!

"If money were no object, I'd live in a pink world. Walls, bed, curtains, furniture. All pink."

the bag lady

Carol is the most unusual collector in this book. Carol collects bags. Not highly coveted designer handbags, oh-so cute purses or hand-beaded evening pouches, but just bags. As in carrier bags. The throwaway items that our shopping collections usually come in.

Carol has collected a huge variety of carrier bags for over twenty years, having begun when her doctor advised her to take up a hobby during a stressful period in her life. She finds collecting, sorting and counting her bags especially relaxing and enjoyable.

Spending around £3 a month on her collection, Carol is always being sent new bags by her friends and family – and is always happy to refund the postage. When relatives left Britain, her collection was further swelled by a cardboard box full of carrier bags "and all they wanted in return was a packet of chocolate eclairs". Even her friends have taken to calling her "the old bag"!

While most of her bags are given to her, she also enjoys scouring Birmingham's rag market and is particularly partial to the limited edition, colourful bags produced by stores at Christmas.

"I love my collection of bags so much that I want them cremated with me when my time's up!"

acknowledgements

My thanks go to all female shoppers everywhere – and that must include virtually every single woman in possession of this book. But especially to all those who were willing to reveal the contents of their wardrobes and show the rest of us their special and unique shopping obsessions. It has been a therapeutic exercise for all of us.

Thanks to Rosemary, Ruth and Yvonne at New Holland and to Laura, Hannah and John for taking the wonderful photographs and making everybody feel so at ease.

And a brief message for any men who may happen upon this book – women love shopping. And shoes. It was decreed thus. It's like the offside rule. We don't expect you to understand or enjoy the exhilaration of each and every shopping trip, but we do expect you to accept it and indulge us and we, in turn, will try our best to do the same for football, rugby, beer or whatever gives you the same passion, enthusiasm and sheer unadulterated pleasure.

The publishers would like to thank Selfridges for allowing us to do a photoshoot in their lingerie department and all those who helped with the research for this book.

By the same author:
The Dating Game; The Little Black Book – both published by New Holland

First published in 2004 by New Holland Publishers (UK) Ltd
London • Cape Town • Sydney • Auckland

Garfield House
86-88 Edgware Road
London W2 2EA
United Kingdom

80 McKenzie Street
Cape Town 8001
South Africa

Level 1, Unit 4
14 Aquatic Drive
Frenchs Forest
NSW 2086
Australia

218 Lake Road
Northcote
Auckland
New Zealand

0 9 8 7 6 5 4 3 2 1

ISBN 1 84330 816 9

Jo Hemmings has asserted her moral right to
be identified as the author of this work.

Editor: Ruth Hamilton
Editorial direction: Rosemary Wilkinson
Production: Hazel Kirkman
Designer: Paul Wright
Photographers: John Baxter, Laura Forrester
and Hannah Mornement

Reproduction by Modern Age repro, Hong Kong
Printed and bound by Craft Print International, Singapore

Photographic Credits
John Baxter: 6; 10; 34-35; 40-41; 46-47; 50-51; 74-75; 84-85; 88-89
Laura Forrester: 9; 13; 20-21; 26-29; 32-33; 36-37; 48-49; 54-61;
68-71; 78-79; 82-83; 86-87; 90-91; 96
Hannah Mornement: Cover – front; Cover – back (top, middle,
bottom); 2; 5; 13; 14; 17; 18-19; 22-25; 30-31; 38-39; 42-45; 52-53;
62-67; 72-73; 76-77; 80-81; 92-93